The Marvelous Kippah

Copyright © 2024 Isabelle Foreman.
All rights reserved. This book is protected under the copyright laws of the United States of America. No part of this book may be reproduced or transmitted in any form or by any means, electronic or mechanical, including photocopying, recording, or by any information storage and retrieval system, without written permission from the author.

ISBN: 9798873070862

First Edition: 2024-Amazon Kindle Direct Publishing
Printed in the United States of America

Book design by Claudia Gadotti
Illustrated by Claudia Gadotti
www.claudiagadottiart.com

In loving memory of
Eugene "Buddy" Foreman (aka Pop Pop)

To Brian and Jake
for all your love and support in following my dreams

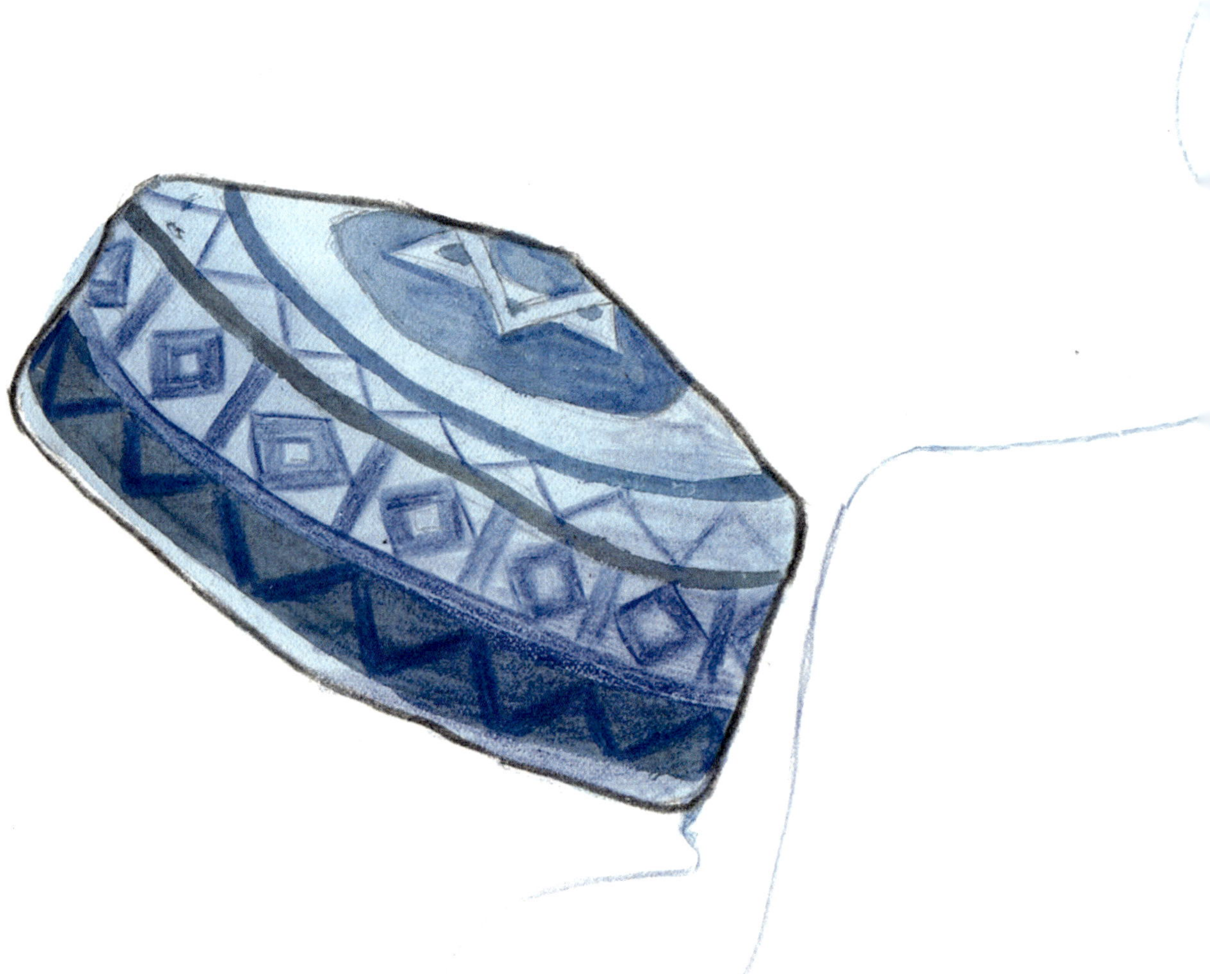

THE MARVELOUS KIPPAH

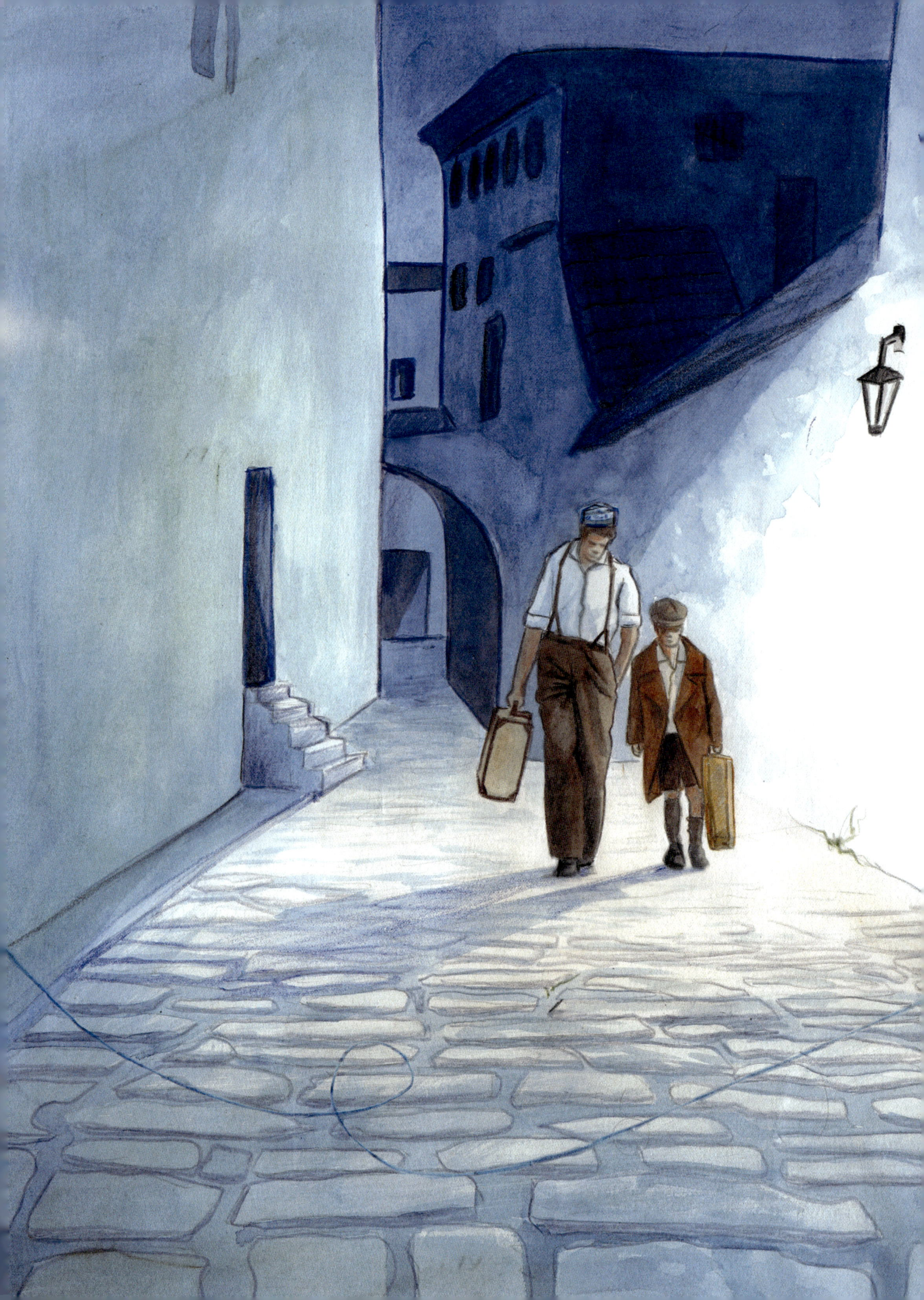

Buddy had a very special kippah passed down to him by his great grandfather. When he wore it, he felt close to his family.

Buddy's grandfather and dad came to the United States as immigrants from Lithuania in 1892. His grandfather packed only a few belongings, but most important, was the marvelous kippah from his grandfather. When he wore it, he felt like his grandfather was watching over him.

Buddy's grandfather told him stories of the long, harsh journey from Europe to Ellis Island, New York. The trip took several weeks on a ship with stormy seas.
There was a shortage of food and a spread of illnesses. When his grandfather felt scared, he touched the marvelous kippah and felt courage.

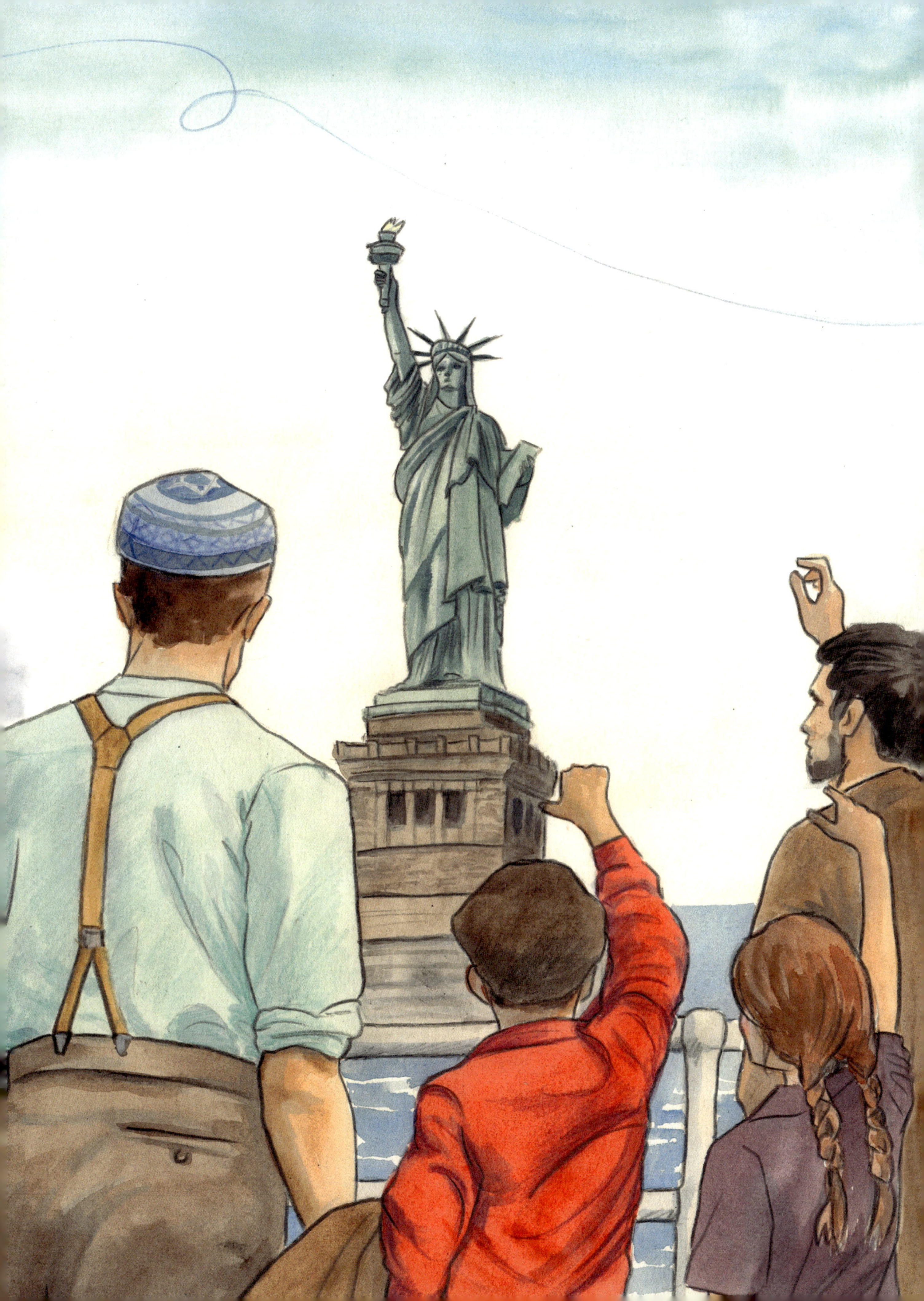

Buddy's grandfather and dad survived the difficult journey and made a new life in Portsmouth, Virginia.
His grandfather and dad opened a small tailor shop and Buddy helped them out by working there after school. When customers brought clothes to be mended, his grandfather told them "If there is one thread left, I can fix it."

His grandfather worked long hours sewing clothes. When he felt tired, he touched the marvelous kippah and felt strength to keep working.

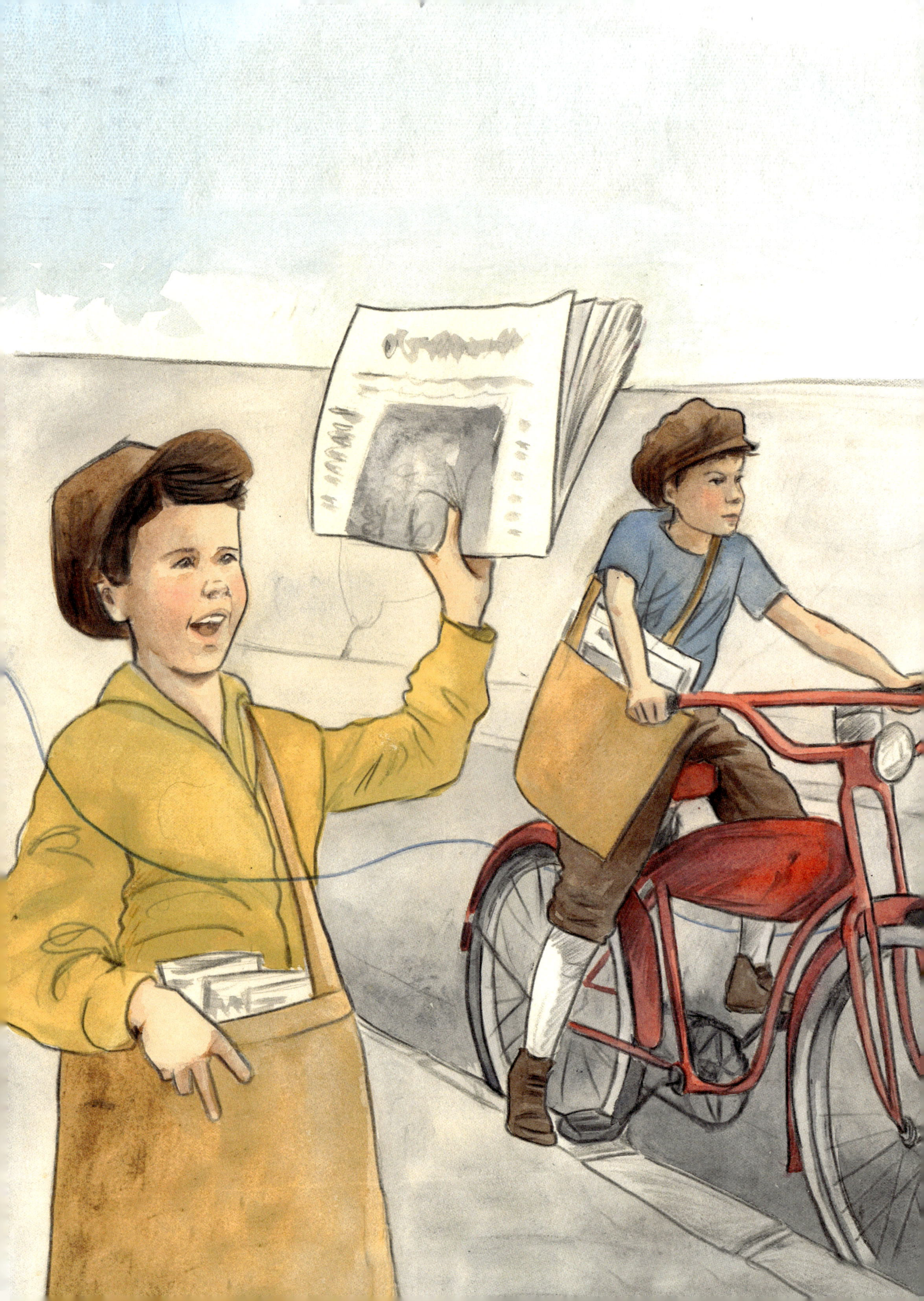

Buddy remembered his family struggling to buy food and heat their home. They shared a 3-bedroom house with their extended family. There were 10 people living in a tiny home with no central heating and only one bathroom. When his grandfather felt despair, he touched the marvelous kippah to feel hope.

Buddy and his family felt they were holding on to survive. Buddy and his brother got newspaper routes to help pay the bills. They woke up early at the crack of dawn to deliver the papers. They each made 25 cents a week and gave all the money to their parents.

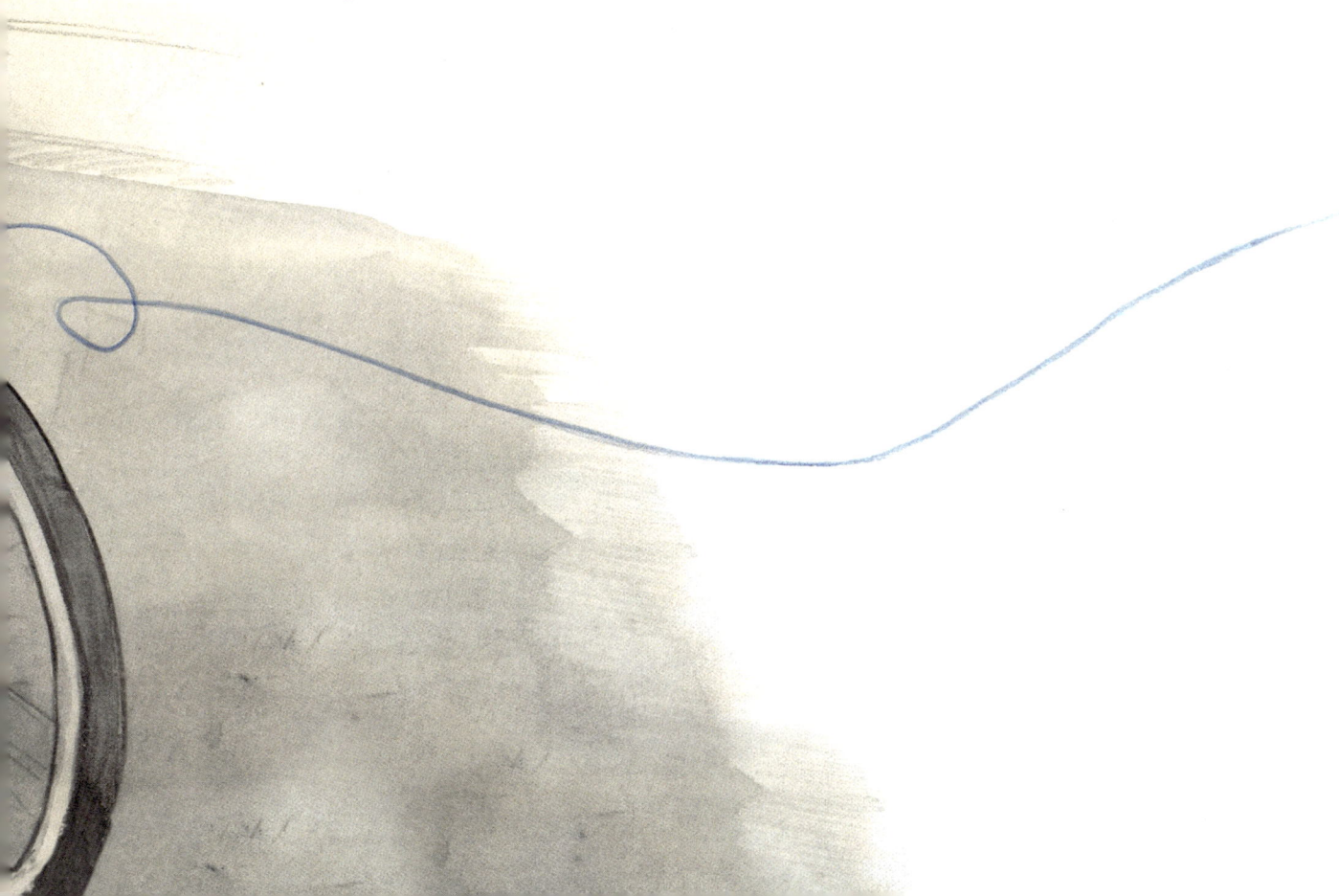

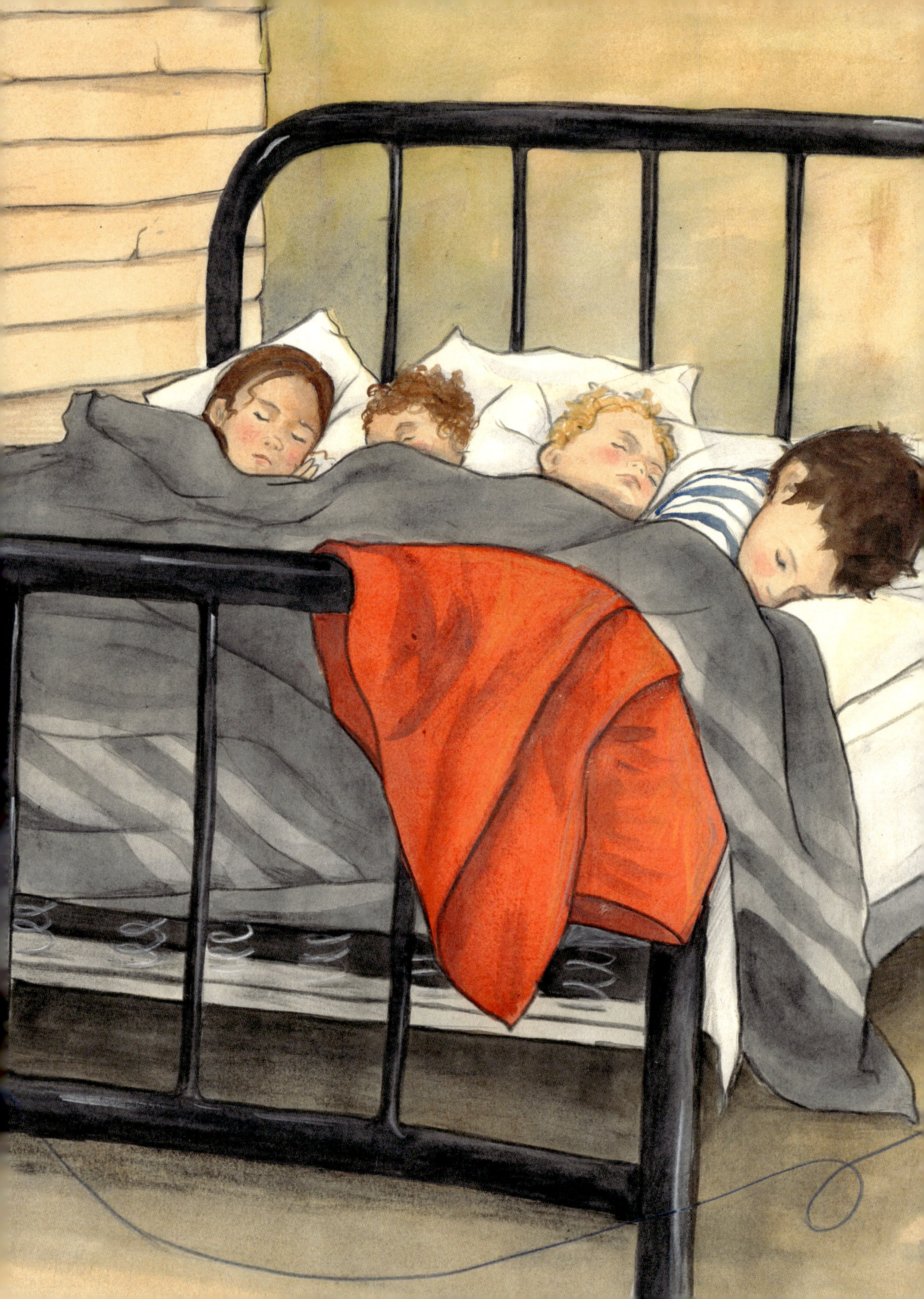

On bitter cold nights, Buddy and his family snuggled under the covers when they were freezing. His grandfather touched the marvelous kippah and prayed for warmth. His prayers were answered when Buddy used the quarters he earned to run the gas meter which heated their home.

Buddy and his relatives shared one small bathroom, so they learned to be patient and wait their turn.

There was only enough hot water to fill one bathtub. So, they took turns using the same tub of water until it turned ice cold.
Buddy thought about the invisible threads that held his family together like the threads of the marvelous kippah. They were poor but happy because they had each other.

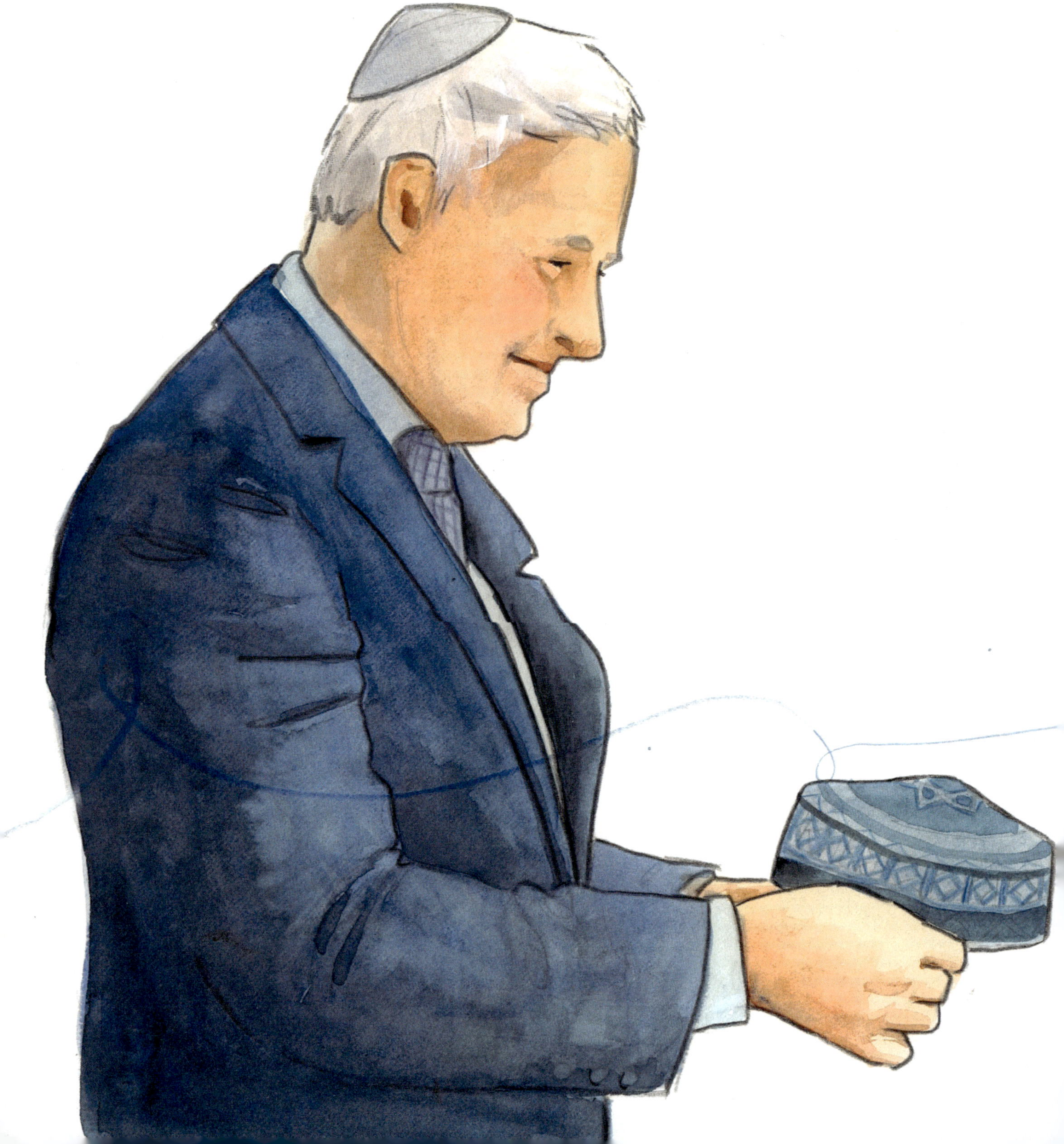

When Buddy turned 13 years old, his grandfather passed on the kippah to Buddy at his bar mitzvah. Buddy treasured the marvelous kippah and felt protected whenever he wore it.

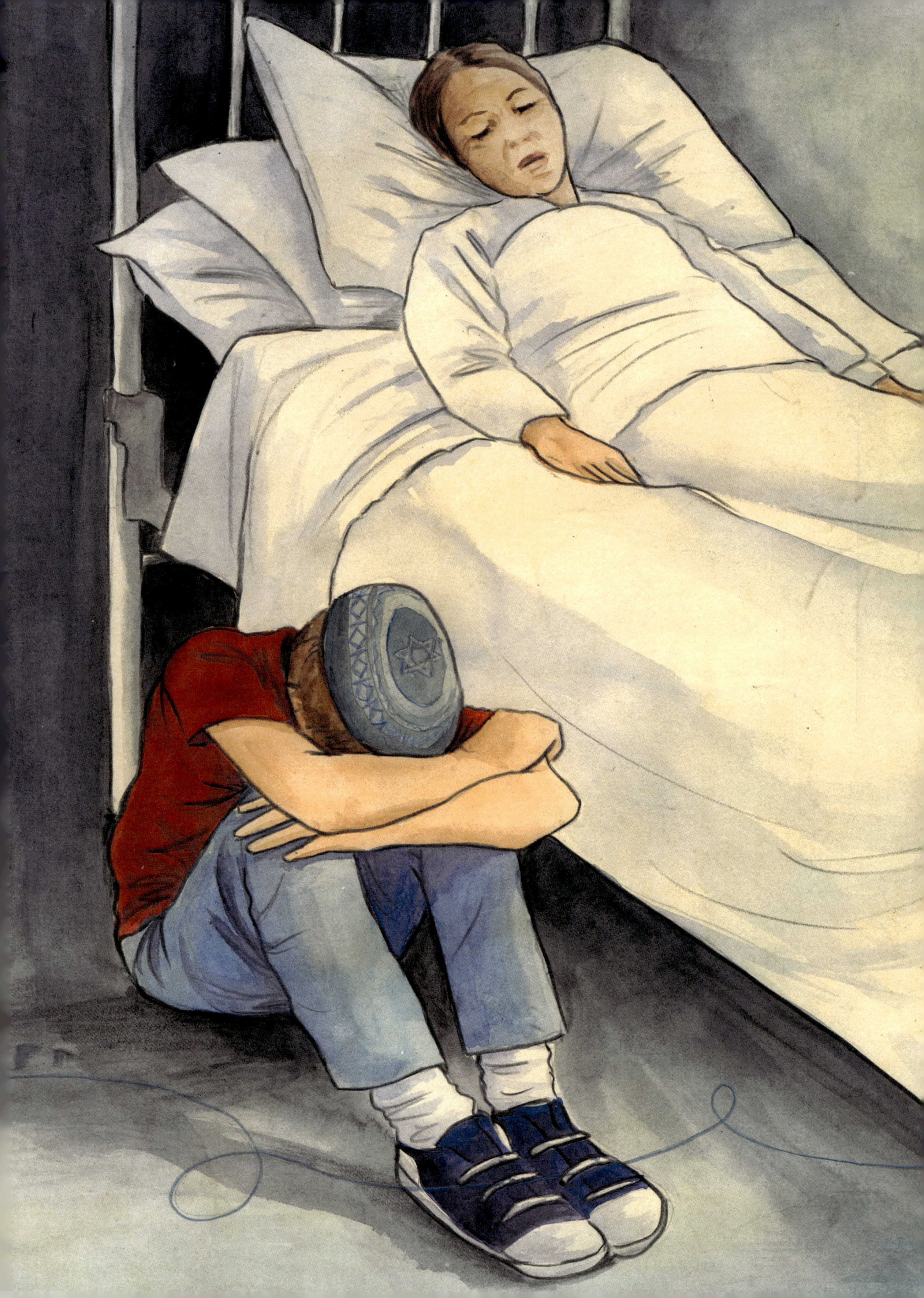

Tragedy struck after Buddy graduated from high school. His mom became ill and unexpectedly died. Buddy was heartbroken. As the tears flowed down his face, Buddy touched the marvelous kippah and felt comfort remembering the special times with his mom.

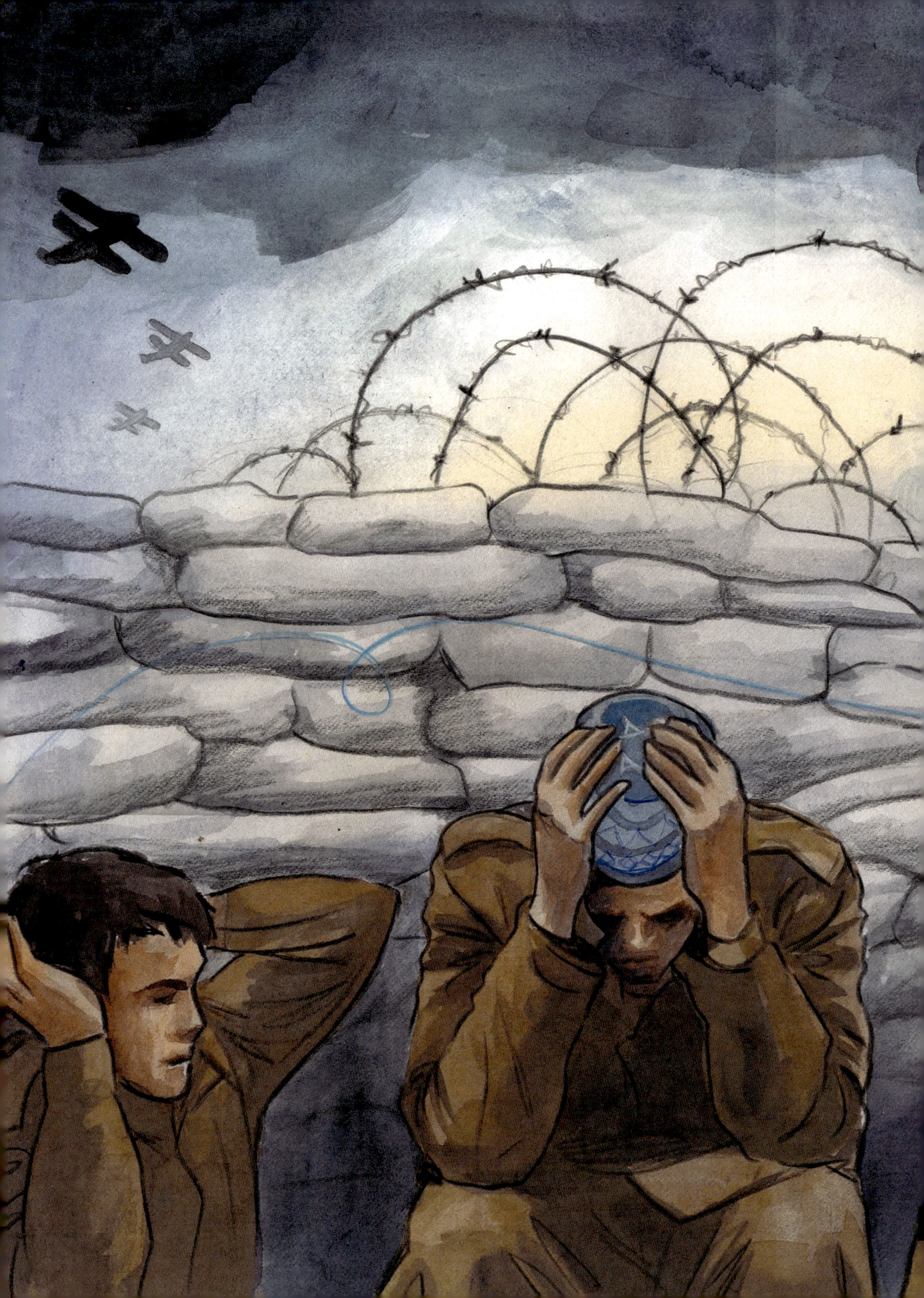

Buddy was drafted into the Army after he graduated from college. World War II was in progress, and he was sent overseas to England. When he heard bombs going off, he felt scared and touched the marvelous kippah to feel safe again.

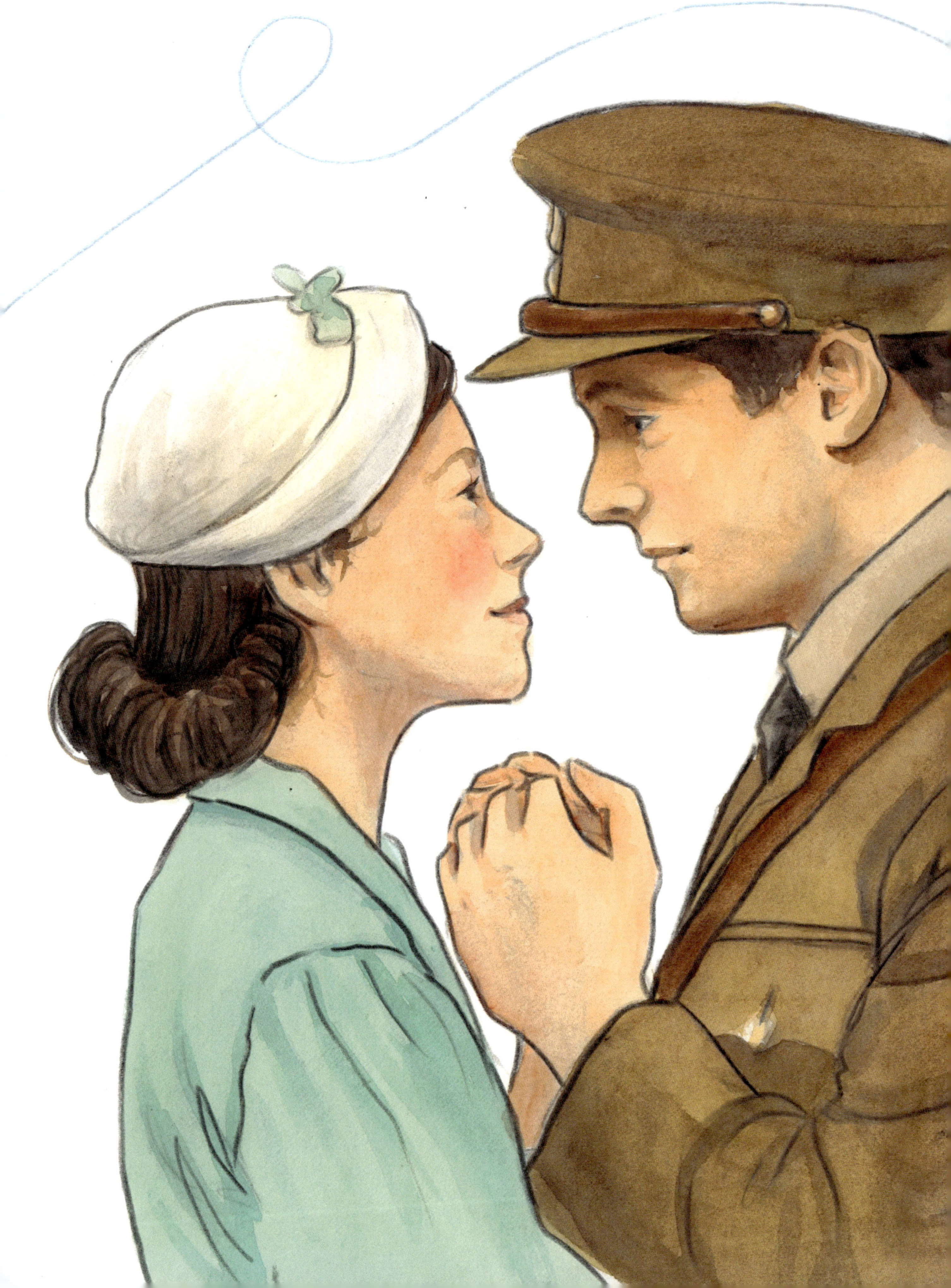

During the war, Buddy often felt lonely being separated from his family. He touched the marvelous kippah and prayed to find true love. His prayers were soon answered. During a short trip back to the U.S., he went on a date with a beautiful woman. Soon after, they married and amazingly Buddy was happily married to the love of his life for 72 years.

Buddy struggled to support his own family. He rode the trolley car to work early each morning because he could not afford to buy a car.

His boss became angry when he arrived late on his first day of work.

He felt discouraged, touched the marvelous kippah, and prayed to find a way to get to work on time.

The next day, his boss lent him money to buy a car.

Through the years, Buddy, his wife, and their four children held together like the threads of the kippah during good and bad times.

Sometimes, he felt like his life was holding on by one thread, but somehow, he was always able to fix it.

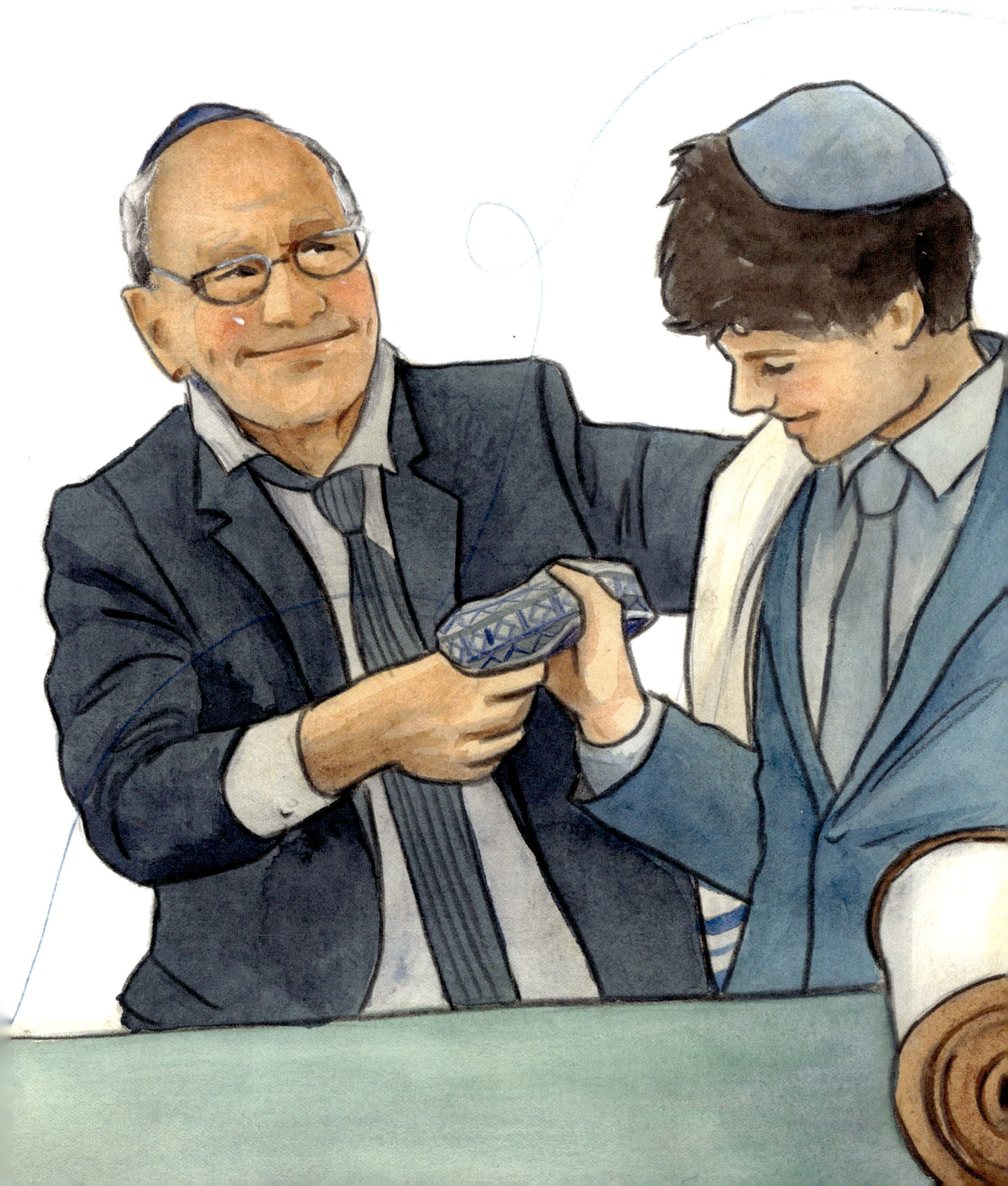

Many years later, 99-year-old Buddy attended his grandson's bar mitzvah. It was a special honor to pass on the marvelous kippah to his youngest grandchild. Buddy told his grandson it is not the material things that matter but the family ties that hold us together forever. Remember the threads of the kippah and if there is one strand of thread left, we can fix it together.

Buddy in his U.S. Army uniform during World War II. He was drafted into the Army on Nov. 27, 1941.

The Marvelous Kippah is based upon the true story of my father-in-law, Eugene "Buddy" Foreman. Buddy had a heart of gold and was the thread that bonded our family together until he passed away at 99 years old. His positive attitude and willingness to always help others was inspiring. We are all part of a rich, colorful quilt that is diverse, yet has many common threads that bind us together despite our differences.

Buddy Foreman and Olga Buchwald's wedding photo. They were married on Feb. 6, 1944 and remained happily married for 72 years.

Buddy at his bar mitzvah in 1933.